CREATIVE HOME DESIGN

BEDROOMS AND BATHROOMS

NONIE NIESEWAND

First published in 1987 by
Stoddart Publishing Co. Limited
34 Lesmill Road
Toronto, Canada
M3B 2T6

Reprinted 1995

Published in Great Britain by
Conran Octopus Limited
37 Shelton Street
Covent Garden
London WC2H 9HN

Canadian Cataloguing in Publication Data

Niesewand, Nonie
    Bedrooms and bathrooms

(Creative home design)
ISBN 0-7737-5737-6

1. Bedrooms. 2. Bathrooms. 3. Interior decoration.
I. Title. II. Series.

NK2117.B4N53 1987   747.7'7   C87-094030-9

Printed and bound in Hong Kong

CONTENTS

BEDROOMS

The bedroom is your personal retreat. Here are kept old teddy bears, soft toys, crumpled clothes – and laundered ones – family photographs, guises and disguises, all revealed to those who enter. Or, if you choose, hidden behind closed doors. Today's bedrooms may be lined with fully fitted cupboards and furniture like a kitchen, or more traditionally furnished with free-standing items such as wooden chests, apothecary drawers, lidded trunks or giant wardrobes. Sometimes these bulky pieces from another age can be updated in the most dazzling way with elaborate paint finishes. Whatever your inspiration, plan your bedroom around its dominant feature – the bed.

Any scheme you envisage must be based on the bed style – a box-spring bed offers a different theme to a four-poster. There are lots of alternatives. You can have a zipped-together double bed that converts easily back into singles (space or partners permitting). At simplest, you can place a mattress on the floor, or on a raised platform. A Japanese futon, a cotton mattress, can be rolled up into a giant bolster by day.

You spend up to a third of your life in bed, so unless you want to become an insomniac, you need a well-supported, comfortable mattress with a firm base. Extra-firm orthopaedic mattresses will suit those with back ailments, and beds that tilt to drop the head lower than the feet are made for those with circulatory complaints. A high-quality foam mattress can be as good, and as expensive, as a sprung mattress, but foam can be hot to sleep upon and must be well ventilated. A futon can be damp unless it is aired every day. Sprung mattresses are heavy and the pocketed-spring varieties are more expensive than interlinked-spring types.

Do not feel inhibited about jumping on to the mattress you have selected before you buy. Lie down upon it, eyes closed, and see if it is comfortable and accommodating. When you lie on a bed, the weight of your body is not evenly distributed across the mattress – your shoulders and pelvis are heavier than your wrists, for example. A good mattress is supple enough to adjust, supports your body weight evenly and makes a firm, flat surface for your back. When buying a double mattress, two people should lie on it side by side to see how firmly it will support two bodies.

PLANNING CHECKLIST

- What size bed suits you?
- Where will you place the bed to leave corridor space and room for opening doors?
- Is the room to have another use? *Consider a sofabed.*
- What are the storage requirements for clothing, linens, luggage, etc:
  - large cupboards
  - drawers
  - hanging rails
  - shelves
  - laundry hamper
  - shoe racks
- Do you prefer built-in or free-standing storage?
- Is the bedroom sunny? *Cooler, north-facing rooms need warming up with decoration.*
- Is the bedroom overlooked? *Curtains also cut down noise.*
- What do you need near the bed:
  - reading light
  - telephone
  - alarm clock
  - radio
  - tea/coffee maker
  - TV/video
  When watching TV, a 355mm (14in) screen should be viewed from at least 1.2m (4ft) away.
- Will you need sockets and space for other activities:
  - sewing machine
  - hair drier
  - typewriter
  - computer

This open-plan bedroom with gallery contrasts traditional with modern styles and natural with primary colours against plain white walls. A bright abstract wall tapestry is set against a stone Regency chimney and the Louis XV armchair is covered with a bright green chintz.

Combination bedroom/work areas in which you entertain, once a symptom of impoverished student times, now may be a sign of freelance work. When furnishing any dual-purpose room, select furniture or design built-ins which will be space-saving and convertible as well as practical. If you need to entertain or conduct business in the room that houses your bed, either use a convertible sofabed or dress the bed to make it a feature of the room.

Good-looking sofas that open up into beds incorporate simple mechanisms that mean you do not have to be an athlete to produce a bed easily when you do want to rest. More elaborate foldaway beds unhinge from the wall, where they pack flat in the best tradition of a James Bond movie. Others concertina outwards, once they have been unscrewed or unbolted.

You can dress an ordinary bed with a fitted cover by day, bolstered with cushions that make it into a deep-seated but adequate sofa. Or you can dress a rather large, dominant bed in such a manner that it is eye-catching. Even a four-poster bed works in a living/dining area: with a kelim rug pinned to the headboard area, canopied in a vivid Bedouin stripe, it looks unusual and essentially nomadic in theme, so it discourages any associations with the boudoir. The satin-sheeted look with its frills and furbelows, which suits some private bedrooms, establishes an embarrassing intimacy, best avoided in combination bedroom/work rooms.

Geometric pinstripes or zany modern designs can be used to good effect on bedcoverings. The patchwork quilt of yesteryear could be revived in the country-fresh interior of an inner-city apartment, designed around simple features like a rag rug, stained floorboards, a stencilled cornice and soft, washed colours.

Platforms provide a change of direction between sleep and work areas. Emphasize this change with different floorings and colours on each level. Bookshelves placed along one side of a platform can double as both a dividing screen and handy storage area for reference works and bedside reading. A desk can also serve as a partition. Or place the desk in a bay or alcove – or even wasted corner space if you can provide adequate light. When the work-load is not so great as to occupy the worktop constantly, consider a foldaway, hinged-top desk that packs flat when you are not working. If you need storage for files, a filing cabinet in new fashion colours can double up as a bedside table.

Constraints of space and budget may dictate your choice of bed to some extent. Within the work environment few other items of furniture meet such a wide range of individual requirements with such diversity. Whatever your bed style, whether a self-indulgent four-poster or a practical built-in platform, it will reflect – and affect – your life style.

1

2

3

1 In dual-purpose bedrooms where there is little space, Japanese futons provide an attractive solution to sleeping and seating, both spacious activities. By day the bedding is rolled or folded so as to become a seating system. Here, a slatted ash double-bed base with red-stained legs supporting two cushioned futon mattresses is converted for daytime use to a low-backed sofa with bolster seating and two coffee-tables.

2 Convertible sofabeds are practical in any room which is used for sitting as well as sleeping. This metal-framed sofabed is upholstered in foam and has a removable quilted cotton cover. It enables this spare room to be used as a studio for a seamstress and also as a guest bedroom and extra sitting room.

3 A restful Japanese-style interior with ivory and eau-de-Nil walls using a futon mattress laid in the traditional way on the floor and a second, rolled-up futon, with a cushion as a back support, used for seating. The only other furniture is an Alvar Aalto stool, an impromptu bedside table for the miniature television. Notice how the light positioned behind the indoor plant tub casts a pool of dappled light and shadow upon the ceiling.

A mattress becomes a bed simply by backing it with cushions or raising it on a built-in platform, or with more traditional bases, headboards and footboards.

1 *The vibrancy of the brilliant bed-linen and high-gloss red storage unit in this low-level bedroom contrasts with the plain white bath visible through the black, glazed doors. The convertible sofabed has a soft yellow backrest for scatter cushions. The storage unit is a good height for watching television in bed.*

2 *This double bed has a sprung base topped with an eighty per cent cotton mattress and a quilted headboard. Co-ordinated detailing makes this conventional bedroom more stylish: the Madras check quilted bedspread matches the drawer fronts and lampshades.*

3 *This unusual attic bedroom combines plain white plasterwork and quarry tiles with black lacquered box shelving and ceiling and brilliant blue bed-linen. A solid concrete slab forms the platform for the double foam mattress. Single Continental quilts allow for individual sleeping habits in a shared bed. The upright concrete slabs of the floor-to-ceiling shelving system and concrete bedside boxes make original built-in furniture.*

4

5

6

4 A pine four-poster bed can be draped to different effect; either with traditional curtains using a fabric such as Bolton twill plus ribbons or sashes, or with sheer muslin draped more simply like a tropical mosquito net. The accessories are suitably Eastern – the Indian dhurry and the ikat design of the bed-linen.

5 A wooden bed, inspired by the simplicity of Quaker design, would fit as well in a smart townhouse interior as it does in this country-style bedroom with its matching sprigged Victorian bed-linen and wallpaper. The curved headboard and footboard are built from traditionally steam-bent solid ash. The bedside table and the chest of drawers come from the same range of furniture as the bed.

6 Different levels, whether sunken or raised, can make a room more attractive. Here, the height of the bedroom floor has been built up to create a platform for a sprung mattress covered in scarlet with a boldly striped extra-large Continental quilt and matching pillows. These can be stashed away by day in deep pull-out drawers at the front of the platform. The fine red architrave line and multicoloured line between white floorboards emphasize the bold stripe of the bedding.

Open-spring mattresses consist of rows of upright wire coils sandwiched between wire frames with padding on top and bottom. The gauge of the wire indicates the resilience of the springs — the higher the gauge, the more giving. This, combined with the number of springs, determines the comfort and durability of the mattress. A double one has about 350 springs.

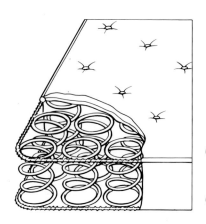
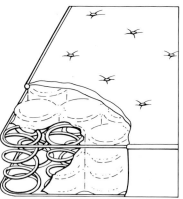

Pocketed-spring mattresses are similar in principle to open-spring mattresses, but each spring is sewn under tension into its own fabric slot or pocket. Because the springs move independently, the mattress is more flexible. Such mattresses incorporate about three times as many springs as open-spring mattresses, so they give more support, but are considerably more expensive.

Foam mattresses vary in quality: the best ones combine layers of foam of different density. A bottom layer of firm foam provides the necessary support, while a softer top layer conforms to individual contours so there are no pressure points. A third outer layer quilted into the mattress cover gives extra cushioning. Foam requires a ventilated base, rather than a solid one.

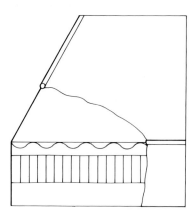
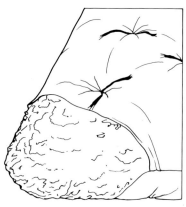

Futons are Japanese mattresses which consist of layers of natural or synthetic fibre, such as cotton or polyester, held in place inside a thick cotton cover with tufted ties. They are available in different thicknesses — generally from 76mm (3in) to 152mm (6in) thick — and some are filled with a mixture of fibres. Futons can be rolled or folded up by day.

1 Traditional brass bed frames are now reproduced in lacquered woods
2 Pocketed-spring mattress on a sprung-edge base
3 Trundle bed with open-spring mattresses and pine frame
4 Bunk bed (stacking twin beds) with open-spring mattresses and solid pine frames

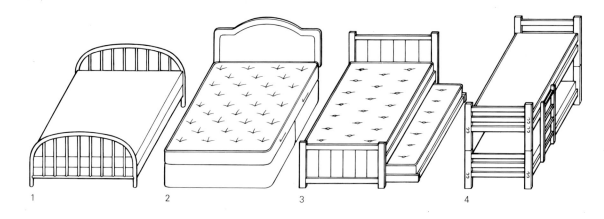

1   2   3   4

Slatted wood bed bases are formed by securely fixing simple softwood slats to a bed frame. It makes a very firm base although it can be quite flexible, as here, where the bed frame is hinged to fold away. A 102mm (4in) foam pad, supported by this slatted wood base, can be folded up when the bed is stored behind a middle cupboard, making a lightweight, space-saving bed.

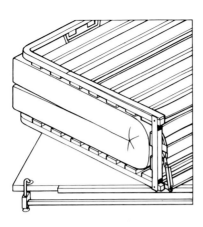

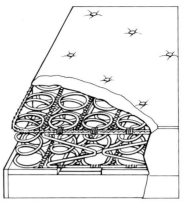

Sprung-edge bed bases consist of rows of upright wire coils supported on a wooden frame, all upholstered with durable fabric. This is the most expensive bed base you can buy. Because the coiled springs extend right out to the edge of the bed base, it is as comfortable to sleep near the edge of the bed as it is in the centre, and there is no tendency to roll inwards.

Sprung slatted wood bed bases, like ordinary slatted bases with firmly fixed softwood slats, tend to be very firm and require an appropriate mattress. An extra degree of give is introduced by sprung hardwood slats held in special flexible fixings. Such a base is not so deep or bulky as a box-like sprung-edge bed base, but is more complex than the ordinary slatted bed.

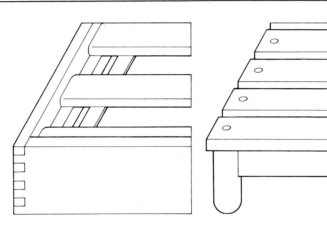

Futon bed bases usually consist of wide wooden slats fixed to a simple, low frame. The slats are closely spaced to prevent the futon from sagging, but narrow gaps are left between the slats to permit air circulation so that it does not become damp or stuffy. Futon bed bases which double as sofa platforms are easy to build, or self-assembly kits can be purchased.

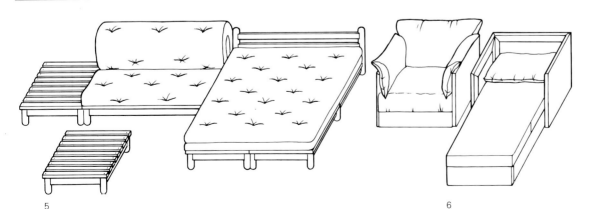

5 Futon sofa made up of two double futons on a platform with two matching side tables converts to a double bed by moving the side tables next to the platform to form a bed base, unrolling the futons and laying them out on the base

6 Convertible armchair with upholstered wooden frame opens into single bed

5

6

The bed occupies more space than any item in your house, including the bath, so how you dress it will determine the style of your room: tailored or casual, quilted or counterpaned, the choice is yours. Only you can decide between the security of familiar sheets and blankets, and the freedom from bed-making that a Continental quilt and fitted bottom sheet brings.

Be it plain or patterned, the top covering will introduce the biggest single jolt of colour to your room. Choose colour schemes wisely for your bed-linen to make a positive statement against the right background. Designer bed-linen provides pattern contrasts: one pattern for the base sheet and a variation for the Continental quilt cover, which is often reversible, with a different yet co-ordinated pillowcase pattern. Use geometric patterns for new angles, with stripes extending the eye visually along the length of the bed or broadening the area in a corridor-like room.

The minimalist who hides clutter behind cupboard doors and prefers to sleep simply upon a floor mattress will choose the purest bed dressing, without intricate patterning and many colours. The simplest is the futon – a Japanese mattress made from tufted cotton wadding layered inside a pure cotton cover. For a modern look, cover a futon with graphic-patterned fabric and top it off with two bolsters akin to Japanese headrests rather than pillows; for a softer effect, choose a pastel futon cover with traditional pillows covered in complementary colours as back- and armrests.

Futons and similar roll-up bedding often fill dual roles, doubling by day as a sofa. Sofabeds themselves seldom provide any daytime storage space for the pillows and coverings, unless you roll and cleat them like yachtsmen's sails to form a bolster. The more expensive convertible sofabeds are upholstered with detachable quilted covers that become the night-time Continental quilt. Or you can take a tip from an architect whose lightweight foam-block mattress is covered in tough but flimsy spinnaker sail fabric made up in all the colours of his studio bedroom. By day, it hangs from the wall and looks like an abstract painting.

The traditionalist will prefer sleeping upon a box-sprung bed raised fairly high from the floor. This bed could have a pleated valance to conceal the legs, and the formality of a fitted bedspread.

Dressing the bed does not end with the bed-linen. You can drape fabric on posts at the four corners or, more simply, create a canopy above with an interesting fabric design to reflect upon when lying in bed. It is possible to make a four-poster bedroom without an actual four-poster bed: hang lightweight curtains from a ceiling rod that matches the bed base in size and shape, or suspend a simple length of fabric, perhaps a hand-blocked Indian sari, between two ceiling rods. You will see many examples on the following pages.

The bed is the centrepiece of
most bedrooms and the largest
object of furniture, so the bed-
linen and coverings are very
important to the finished effect
of the whole room. Here, the
simple effect of a neatly folded
blanket emphasizes the lines
of the bed against the curves
of the unusual arched windows.
The blue and yellow tones
marry beautifully with the hazy
blue walls and silk Indian rug.
Dressed in this simple way, the
bed can be easily matched
with plain and inexpensive
furniture such as these small
tables and foldaway chairs for a
casual breakfast or informal
study area.

Bed-linens can determine both the colour scheme and mood of a room. Frills and flounces with valances and counterpanes say something individual about you. When the colour scheme has already been established, with painted or papered walls, and floor coverings laid, take colour samples with you when choosing bed-linen. If you start from scratch, the range of sheets, covers and pillowcases makes it possible to plan the room around the bed-linens you like best, distributing the colours of the linens across the background.

1 *A cool blue lightweight cover with neatly mitred corners around striped sheets suits this restful room with little for contemplation but some collectors' ceramics and two abstract paintings. The low-level bed, with its curved black tubular headboard and frame, blends with the black lacquer furniture to give the room style.*

1

2

3

2   *In this theatrical Japanese bedroom dressing, the double scale of small chequerboard pillowcases and Continental quilt cover set against giant squares dramatizes the black and white theme. The Japanese style is carried through the paper and wooden panelling at the windows, the tatami matting used on the bed platform and the Japanese Noh theatre puppets strung up on the walls.*

3   *Here adventurous bed-linen transforms a basic box-bed. Geometric stripes, cleverly combined in changes of colour, direction and weight, are mirrored to make a double image. Red and white stripes anchor the box-springs, mattress, bedspread and pillows, all covered with the same width yellow and white stripes, and they are balanced by the fine-line blue and white horizontal stripe on the twin chairs standing against the facing wall.*

Three types of bedcover, all set against plain flooring and walls, traditional wooden furniture and simple window treatments, suggest ways of capturing country style in a town or country bedroom. Country style depends upon a certain understatement in design and an honest, undisguised admiration of form and handicraft to achieve its freshness and charm.

1 A traditional American quilt turns the bed into the decorative centrepiece of this room. The quilted pattern of green leaves and red flowers is picked up by the red scatter cushions, small potted geraniums and decorative frieze on the white blinds. Next to the beautifully inlaid old headboard stand tall wicker baskets, which make unusual bedside tables.

2 This simple room quaintly mixes a floral print with unfussy stripes. The patterned fabric gathered into a valance for the bed is also used for a tablecloth and the cushion on the white rattan chair. The fine muslin cotton quilt is striped in the same warm colours, and the floral motif appears again in the painting used as a fireplace screen, the old embroidered tablemat framed above the fireplace and the jugs or vases of flowers on every surface.

1

2

3

3 Even a Continental quilt and pillowcases with a relatively modern, abstract line design can look serenely countrified on a wooden bed. The soft colours tone with the rug, tiles, and walls painted a creamy pink. The country feel is followed through in details: the framed sampler, candlesticks upon the pine surround, the pitcher with flowers and the wooden stationery box on the little dresser under the window.

Continental quilts (known as comforters or duvets) are an alternative to sheets and blankets, which simplify bed-making. Channels filled with a natural or synthetic insulating fibre comprise the quilt within the cover, made from cotton or sheeting fabric to complement the pillowcases and bottom sheet. Natural fillings are light and warm: goose down is the most luxurious filling, although a mixture of duck down and feather is cheaper. Synthetic fillings are easy to launder, hard-wearing and suitable for those who are allergic to natural feathers.

Using fabric drapes over a bed makes the bed the focal point, as elaborate and eye-catching as any decorative window treatment or drape.

1 *This wooden four-poster bed with a lattice-work bed base is built around a recessed window, using a fringed Turkish bed hanging embroidered in silver for drapes. The bed is painted in the same traditional pale blue used for the built-in furniture, wooden frames and stair-rail.*

2 *A generous length of a delicate material like muslin, voile, cambric or even window netting makes economical but theatrical drapes, with a touch of fun added here by the loosely tied red ribbons which attach the material to the ceiling and allow it to fall into a canopy. The covered headboard and quilted bedcover are patterned in the same colours as the rag rug.*

3 *A luxury bed has been created in a small bedroom by hanging sumptuous modern drapes from the ceiling and placing an eighteenth-century headboard against the wall. The ruched backcloth, canopy and self-lined curtains are suspended from an upholstered tester with no posts. The matching, broadly quilted bedspread and crewel-work cushions are in silk cambric.*

1

2

3

4 This bed drape with a colonial air is achieved by splitting a mosquito net two-thirds of the way up its circular shape so it can be drawn back and the ends knotted around cleats at either side of the bed. The unadorned wood panelling is offset by the plain bed set in a white box and by the window frames. The style of this tropical bedroom can equally be used in northern climates with central heating – a ceiling fan circulates warm air around the room.

5 This small four-poster bed in a mountain inn in the French alps was built by local craftsmen. Its broad border fringing the poles is pulled taut to show the frieze-like pattern of lace flowers. The plump Continental quilt is covered by plain white bed-linen.

6 A curtain swathed over poles at the head of the bed, here enclosing two lacquered rattan bedside tables, lends a classical touch to a modern bedroom. The squared silk moiré scatter cushions lift the richly patterned apricot fabric used for the bedspread, headboard and drapes.

Many of us actually live in the bedroom – or should we say, sleep in the living room? Such a room can be variously known as a studio, a bedsit, a one-room apartment, or an open-plan space – depending on its size and grandeur. These rooms by their very nature contain the whole range of activities of their occupants' lives, and must be much more carefully planned and decorated than any other type of interior. Organization is the key to one-room living.

The average bedroom is often used for dual purposes since few can afford the luxury of a separate room for every activity. The bedroom is the obvious place for study, exercise, hobbies, mending, for TV viewing in luxuriously comfortable surroundings or even a professional home office.

A clear principle for a room with multiple functions is to ensure that it may be cleared of one when you wish to do the other. The one-room home must contain a bed that disappears from sight when not in use, or doubles as a sofa. The popular folding sofabed, which comes in a wide range of styles and prices, is a good solution for one-room living, guest rooms and those bedrooms which serve as a home office. Some fitted storage walls include a pull-down bed behind a panel, with shelves on either side.

Another essential element in the dual-purpose room is efficient and adequate storage so that the room does not become cluttered and unmanageable. Storage can be an integral part of the room's style – an attractive free-standing wardrobe can look charming in a period studio and, similarly, a filing cabinet will not look out of place in a modern room with a tubular steel platform bed. Plan for co-ordination as well as function.

It is worth listing all the functions of the room and with them the accessories, equipment and items to be used or stored there. This list will make it easy to draw up a detailed ground plan for the room on graph paper so that each object is carefully positioned. Make a clear distinction between different activities, so that one does not intrude upon the other. Flexibility is the key word. Objects or fittings which themselves have double functions are both useful and space-saving: if, for example, you choose a desk select one which can serve as a dining table.

Window dressing and lighting must be flexible, too. A bedroom requires privacy from the outside world and shade from intrusive early morning sunlight. But ensure that the windows can be fully revealed if the daytime room is a home office or a living room with its full quota of possible sunlight. After consideration of bedroom lighting, remember that other activities and products have their own requirements, such as home computers where light must not shine directly on the screen, or into the eyes of the operator, or studio entertaining where seating and tables must be subtly illuminated.

A practical space-saving bed can become a design feature: by day, the base slides away on castors under a large seating platform with cushions. The platform is deep enough to hold the Continental quilt and pillow in the wooden bed frame, with a smaller adjacent drawer for bed-linen and space for general storage.

The room is made light and spacious for daytime living by the colour scheme – with white and cream walls, floor, ceiling, print and unlined curtains. Reflected light comes from mirrored wardrobe doors and a sleek swivel pivot chrome lamp gives electric light wherever it is needed. Plants use the height of the room to full advantage while occupying very little precious floor space.

Any sleeping space which doubles as a private work or general living area, either relaxed or formal, needs clever design and furnishings so that the room can move between day and night use.

1 *One-room living often requires bed-linen which breaks with traditional bedroom cosiness to make the right daytime effect. Either hide the bed-linen by day, transforming the bed into a more formal day-bed, or choose bed-linen that looks discreet. Here, the formal restraint of the neatly striped covers, set against a black valance and pillow support, links perfectly with the modern severity of the leather chairs, coffee-table and lamp beyond. The thinly striped grey curtains, exotic plants and modern table and light used at the bedside also help to unify the room.*

1

2

3

2 In this imaginative conversion of a small space into a bedroom with work area the neat twin desks, with a clip-on photographer's light, are supported by the bed frame, which also contains a slide-out storage drawer. A deep wall-to-wall shelf around the side and back of the built-in bed makes a surface for television, plants and ornaments and another above the bed at ceiling level provides storage. The floor-to-ceiling wall mirror and uniformly white decor, with the Venetian blinds echoed by horizontally striped wallpaper, create the illusion of more space.

3 The most effective, but also the most expensive, solution to the problem of space is a bed which folds up behind a wood-finish door as part of a wall shelf and storage unit. The bed closes away with mattress and bedding, and the spring mechanism and lightweight frame make it easy to use.

Careful planning can turn cramped dual-purpose bedrooms into comfortable and efficient studio-style workplaces.

1 *A large drawing table and a work desk are fitted into space released by lifting the bed to a height that also accom- modates a large storage cabinet in this teenage room. The matching red filing cabinet under the desk, the red anglepoise lamp and quilt form links between the sleep and work areas, standing out against the neat white walls, shelving and window shutters.*

2 *This screened desk on wheels provides a large, mobile writing surface that can be rolled around on the hard-wearing jute floor. The easily enclosed corner with bedside table also gives access to a neatly designed storage cupboard with sliding doors that need no clearance space. The dual purpose of this room is reflected in the conical wall lamp giving a soft bedroom light and the supplementary reading light on the desk.*

1

2

3

FITTING FOLDING SHELVES

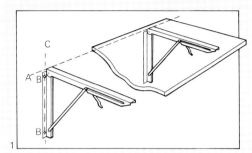

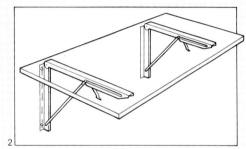

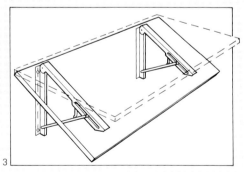

A shelf which folds against the wall can be immensely useful in a small bedroom which doubles as a work room, and is easy to install on folding brackets: **1** Use a spirit level to ensure that positions A, B and C for the brackets and shelf are correctly marked. Holes B should line up vertically. When they are marked, drill and plug the wall and screw on the brackets. **2** Screw the shelf or table on to the brackets. **3** The special brackets lock into an upright position when the shelf is lifted for use.

3 *A bedroom can also double well as a sewing room: the hinged sewing table folds flat against the wall when not in use, with sewing equipment stashed away in wide white shelves, in undershelf baskets and hooked on a wire board, all compactly arranged on the upper wall. The full-length pine-framed mirror is also useful for dressmaking. The shuttered windows and lamp with flexible neck provide plenty of light, for working by day or night, and the stencil border picks up an embroidery motif.*
Visible wall-mounted storage, such as a hook-and-pegboard system or wire-grid system like this, can be immensely versatile, since hooks, clips, shelves and trays can be added to hang almost any tool or utensil within easy reach. Hiding clothes is a priority; transforming the large space taken up by the bed into an unobtrusive area is another. Planning the worktop — be it draughtsman's board, sewing table or just a plain desk — to be both readily available, yet not a nagging or challenging feature, is the next.

Bedrooms in modern houses are seldom larger than 3m × 3.7m (10ft × 12ft) yet they contain an enormous amount. Personal belongings, winter and summer clothing, shoes, valuables and bedding are all kept in bedrooms, behind the closed doors of fitted units, or in free-standing furniture.

Fitted bedrooms look smart, but do not necessarily save space. When built-in furniture lines an entire wall length, that amount of floor space narrows the room dimensions accordingly. By comparison, a free-standing wardrobe or a chest of drawers takes up less overall space, but requires more free floor space in front for opening doors or pulling out drawers.

Free-standing wardrobes and chests of drawers in the generous sizes of another spacious era are often inherited. Unconventional storage solutions come from designers who use shop-fitters' furniture, from fashion-shop swing rails to garage mechanics' tool-box trolleys. Extendable arms used in hospitals have been re-employed as domestic bedside tables so the telephone, TV or books can be brought quickly to hand and as swiftly replaced when needed.

Lidded wicker baskets, old school trunks and pull-out boxes on castors that roll beneath the bed are just some of the more solid pieces that can house bedding, providing a linen chest for winter blankets and Continental quilts in the hot months.

When not used for seating, a chair or a day-bed can serve as an impromptu clothes support and blanket throw. A three-panel screen, covered with fabric or paper scraps, offers privacy for dressing as well as somewhere to hang clothes.

To assess the need for a working wall of fitted furniture, use chalk to mark out the spaces along the wall for wardrobes and drawers to the measurements specified in a manufacturers' catalogue. Marketed in pack-flat kits, these units can be self-assembled, though the more expensive ranges on adjustable plinths need specialist fitting. Features like corner carousel racks, stacking shoe racks, containers for storing out-of-season clothes in the inaccessible upper parts, concertina doors that save space, built-in lighting or even a safe for valuables can be housed inside.

The façade presented by fitted furniture doors will determine the look of the bedroom, depending on the finish you choose, whether rustic pine, limed oak, bold lacquered colours or scumbled, dragged or spattered fashion-paint finishes. The more expensive door fronts feature detailed mouldings – make your own by glueing on painted picture-frame edgings or split bamboo bought by the metre. Interior designer John Stefanides uses sections of ordinary garden trellis, painted and tacked to massive cupboard fronts, then given a moulded edging, as a way of cheaply breaking up a façade of faceless door fronts.

This loft bedroom combines rural simplicity with a careful attention to architectural detail. The furnishings and furniture – tapestry headboard, old painted metal console and loosely draped armchair – are simple but decorative. The panelling and chimney-alcove cupboards have moulded fronts, picked out in white against the grey stippled doors, and a black keyhole motif.

Unfitted storage requires space, but need not dominate the room if properly spaced and highlighted to blend or contrast with the period and decorative scheme of a room.

1 *This steely grey and charcoal monotone room relies largely on an unfitted storage system, but remains visually uncluttered. The versatile trolley, which can be pushed around, here becomes a television table with a lower version used as a bedside table. The tall tubular steel tower with fixed perforated shelves has space for books or tall ornaments. The only fitted storage — the blocked-up fireplace shelved for a stereo system and speakers — and the bare hanging rail are left open to complement the unadorned steel frame furniture, but they could be covered with curtains or slatted wooden blinds.*

2 *A free-standing coat rack provides unconventional but space-saving hanging space. It becomes a decorative feature in an otherwise conventionally furnished bedroom. The wigwam-shaped rack makes a good use of alcove space and links well with the black-painted grate surround of the old fireplace.*

3

3 An advantage of using free-standing storage is that it introduces some attractive items of furniture into the bedroom. These bentwood chairs would not look as good in a room of wall-to-wall cupboards, but they are very much at home with the old wooden chest of drawers. In a room such as this, with an atmosphere and charm of its own – resulting from the fact that it is an attic with a sloping ceiling, old window and wooden ladder up to a skylight – a modern, stylized, bedroom system would spoil that charm. However, such considerations must be weighed against the storage requirements. No bedroom will please the eye if it is constantly cluttered with objects that have no home.

Fitted storage units neatly house clutter behind old-fashioned panelling suited to period rooms, spartan hi-tech metal from a gym, or sliding white doors. It is important that the interior fittings accommodate everything you need to store – shoes, socks and underwear, hanging garments, folded clothes, even spare suitcases – as it is to select a system to complement the decor you have chosen.

1 Floor-to-ceiling storage such as this leaves stored clothes easily viewed on heavy-duty shelves built from standard lengths of vinyl-coated steel wire shelving. The clothes rack, built in under the top shelf, and the shoe storage unit provide the other necessary components for a highly flexible unit that fits inside a cupboard recess or alcove, protected by a louvred door or a more conventional door. You could screen it with a curtain.

1

2

3

FITTING ADJUSTABLE SHELVING

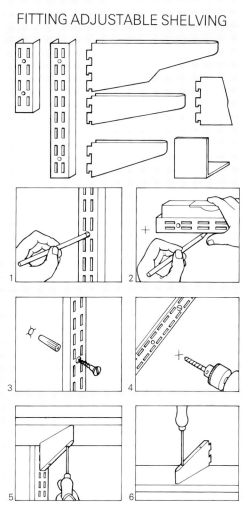

1 Hold upright supports to wall and mark fixing hole.
2 Using spirit level and straight-edge, mark identical fixing holes for adjacent uprights. **3** Drill, plug and screw at each mark. **4** Make sure upright is vertical. Mark other fixing holes. Loosen screw, swing upright sideways, then drill, plug and screw marked positions. **5** Slot brackets into uprights and position shelf on top. Screw shelf to bracket (uppermost shelf first), or **6** mark through brackets, remove to screw shelf and bracket together, then slot back into upright in one piece.

2 This fitted storage unit combines cupboards with beaded panelling and glass doors custom-made to complement the cornice and moulding of the eighteenth-century room. Painted in pale apricot and white, with pleated fabric matching the wallpaper, the small open-shelving islands at either end of the unit give it a decorative touch. The bed base is also hand painted in the same pale apricot, emphasized with white mouldings, but the hand-marbled panelling lends a variety of colour and texture that tones with the sky-patterned carpet and striped wallpaper.

3 Ventilated gymnasium locker cupboards make an unusual domestic storage system that fits perfectly in this modern bedroom, stripped to bare essentials. It has sanded and waxed floorboards, a mattress with black and white paned covers simply laid on the floor and four spotlights on wires extended from a central lighting point along a line across the cupboards. One wall is mirrored like a gymnasium, and another has been speckled with cream and a grey-green paint to match the cupboards.

Wall-to-wall storage, varied in both form and style, is used like an extended plan chest as a platform under a bed, built into awkwardly angled walls to make use of dead space or ranged behind Japanese screens. It provides the extended storage space often needed for dual-purpose bedrooms, leaving space around the bed and creating an open, uncluttered atmosphere.

1 *The awkward shape of an attic has here been emphasized by the storage system rather than treated as a problem. The unit was assembled at home from a system made of individual components varying in shape, size and colour. It combines tall full-length cupboards and vertically stacked shelving that follows the slope of the eaves with an L-shaped bar of cupboards and shelves which double as a headboard and room divider. The shape of the room is further highlighted by the grey carpet following the line demonstrated by the lower storage unit and the muslin cover battened to the recess of the skylight.*

1

2

3

2 *Custom-built storage need not be prohibitively expensive. It offers an opportunity to create an unusual and stylish element in the room. These cupboards are based on Japanese room dividers. They demonstrate the importance of building such structures from floor-to-ceiling as well as wall-to-wall because they then create a complete wall rather than a fussy or irregular section in the room. Another clever device here is the screen on the window which matches the paper 'screening' on the cupboard doors and further unifies the room. Natural wood floors, bamboo table and plain walls are the perfect accompaniment to the Japanese style.*

3 *Since a bed does not need any great depth of ceiling, the floor level may be built up even when there is no high ceiling. This arrangement creates a large deep-drawer storage chest and clearly defines the bed area as a spacious place, suitable for daytime relaxation and sleep. The quilted fitted bottom sheet and Continental quilt, with its reversible cover that matches the bed base and sheet, lend a luxurious touch, while the platform space around the bed allows everything necessary to be at a convenient level alongside, while providing drawers underneath.*

General bedroom lighting involves creating atmosphere with fittings that complement the decorative scheme. To find the right level and quantity of light for bedroom activities, you need a dimmer switch to control the level of intensity. Otherwise, lighting may be too harsh, without softness of play between light and shade. Although pendant or hanging lights are often used, they are obtrusive and flatten shadows. Wall washers will give a less intense light than down-lighters, which should be used sparingly in the bedroom. An awkward placing can glare. Unlike most other rooms, here you will be viewing the lights from flat on your back and you should therefore site them accordingly.

Bedside lighting is crucial and can prove problematic. Whether you are gripped by a spine-chilling thriller or catching up on the Sunday paper, you do not want the page you are reading plunged into shadow when you change position. You may wish to dim the reading light at times so it can double as atmospheric background illumination, and will certainly want to be able to switch it on and off easily from the bed and find the switch in the dark. Free-standing lamps provide numerous small light sources, while purpose-built fittings direct the light exactly where it is needed, with a shade diffusing the light. Avid late-night readers who do not wish to disturb the sleep of others can also try the ultimate in personal reading lights – a very small, high-intensity lamp mounted on a large clip which clamps on to the book itself to illuminate each page.

More than most windows, bedroom windows need to be well protected against any passerby's gaze. Privacy is vital. Just as dimmers control the intensity of light by night, so blinds filter daylight. By lowering or raising them, you change the intensity of the light. Window treatments of every conceivable type are possible: from lined drapes to light-filtering nets, from shirred festoons to trimmed Roman blinds, from louvred shutters to paper panels.

Desks in the bedroom are often placed at the window, so keep windows clear with an efficient window blind that rolls away by day. Anyone living in a high-rise apartment with a small child and outward-opening windows should consider installing vertical window bars for the first few years of the child's life, which are less likely than horizontal bars to become a hazardous climbing frame. In a child's room, light on desktops is essential to focus on the work at hand, but trailing wires should be avoided. Colourful clip-on photographers' lights which can be moved at will, clipped on to work surfaces and set at right angles, are a popular choice, as the illustrations of the real-life rooms featured in the book show. Track-mounted spotlights above a pinboard or mirror provide light where it is most needed. Safety lights and low-level light switches are helpful for young children who may be nervous of the dark.

Bedroom lighting requirements vary. General overhead light is a basic requirement to replace daylight by night or when drapes are drawn, while additional task lighting for dressing, making-up, hairdressing or reading – even working – needs to be considered. A dimmer switch which controls the intensity of light to suit the mood can be invaluable in a bedroom. Simply, shades can vary the direction and intensity of light. One solution to reading in bed without sufficient light is a metal hospital light specifically designed for bedridden people so it can be extended, angled and adjusted as required. Created to last and work effectively, it has been given a high-quality metal finish in a simple design.

1 This room is impressive for its sheer size, original architectural details and abundance of natural light. The bed is placed to take full advantage of unusually large bay windows. Discreet, narrow, fitted Venetian blinds do not interrupt the fine frames or detract from the generous proportions of the bay. They allow for maximum sunlight and enjoyment of a leafy view, but also give sufficient privacy when necessary. The moulding on the cornices and the geometric lines of the parquet floor can be appreciated against bare walls and simple furniture. Blocking off a corner behind the bed creates a headboard and provides a neat shelf for personal mementoes.

1

2

2 *Another bed area has been created in a spacious room, this time a dark alcove rather than a sunny bay. It has the quality of a private, cosy retreat, screened from the room and its battered day-bed by a full-length white curtain. Lighting for the alcove adds to its peaceful seclusion because only low-level fittings are used, rather than glaring overhead illumination. Two small lamps on the bookcase and bedside lights provide a warm glow against the deep ochre shade of the walls. This colour also separates the bed area from the main room and assists the intimate warm atmosphere. Red chair seats enhance the wall colour as does the deep tone of the bedspread.*

Bedroom windows pose particular problems for the decorator. Nobody wants their bedroom overlooked, yet excessive privacy with muffled or screened windows is stifling. Window dressing needs imagination.

1 Rich, embroidered fabric, elaborately styled, provides a grand feeling in this traditional bedroom. The curtain and pelmet form a decorative frame to the windows. Privacy is provided by net blinds which gather into festoons when raised. The bed is also framed with drapes in a heavy plain pink material; the use of decorative fabric is repeated on the bedspread and with the floral print of the bed-linen. Every object has been chosen for its traditional dignity – the gilt mirror, table lamps, silver boxes and candlestick, old polished wood tables and a small, ornamental wall table below the mirror carrying an antique china dog and a small print of a cherub.

2 This cottage bedroom has matching sprigged wallpaper and blinds and a pleasing design which props the blind away from the window so that it forms an awning over a traditionally styled chest in natural wood finish.

2

3

4

3 The recessed window in an old cottage has been used to create a pleasant study area in a bedroom where the view can be appreciated. By choosing a table which fits the recess, the work area is clearly defined, flooded by natural light during the day and lit by a simple table lamp at night. The floral curtains are in keeping with the cottage atmosphere and frame the area attractively.

4 Roman blinds in plain white cotton give a fresh clean style to windows. They are not formal or fussy but provide a neat finish to the room, particularly where there is a large expanse of windows. The blinds gather, when raised, into large folds and, when lowered, look similar to roller blinds detailed with battens. The white backdrop against which the bedspread, the greenery of the plants and the leafy garden beyond can be viewed provides texture and colour. Blinds are used in the same way as the plain white carpet and walls.

More than in any other room of the house, lighting in the bedroom must be specific. You need light for reading, for dressing, for applying make-up – and a single overhead general light will not do the task. Most people buy bedside reading lights, usually a pair of standard table lamps with a white paper shade, perhaps pleated or border-trimmed, whose deflecting cone shape casts a wider light. Some beds have built-in reading lights attached to the headboard which save reaching out for cords and switches. Or two overhead wall lights can be fixed at the top two corners of the bed, each with its own switch, and angled to illuminate the page. Make sure you attach any such light high enough so that it does not pose a hazard for someone sitting up in bed. Some of the newest low-voltage halogen lights which burn brightly for hours from a single small bulb are so tiny that they can fit on to a book page, a bedside tray or on to a headboard clamp.

Another area which requires specific lighting is the mirror. This is notoriously difficult, and is hardly solved by the traditional manufacturers' inclusion of a strip fluorescent light above vanity mirrors. Actors' dressing rooms have naked bulbs ringed around the mirror, which light the sides of the mirror and reflect a more flattering appearance.

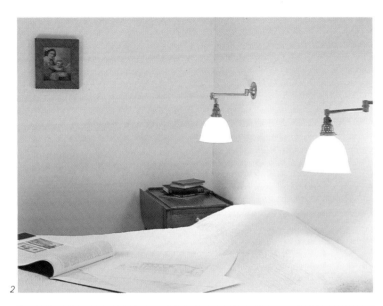

2

3

BEDROOM LAMPS

Solid brass wall light with swinging arm and paper shade

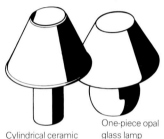

Cylindrical ceramic lamp

One-piece opal glass lamp

Polished brass wall bracket

Spring-clamp lamp can clip on to book or shelf

Unshaded opaque round wall lights

1 *White on white classic bed-linen decorated with lace and embroidery and a bedspread with a woven pattern is highlighted under a low-level table light at night. The windows and walls are unified with matching wallpaper and fabric for the blind, co-ordinated by the green window frame and matching trim to the blinds.*

2 *In a very simple room, a pair of brass and glass wall lights provide reading light as well as general illumination for the room. They are a feature in themselves because of the prominence they are given by the bare walls. It is important to consider whether a light fitting is to be a prominent feature in a room because it must then work in harmony with other objects. These lights are well matched by the painting in a wooden frame and the wooden side table.*

3 *In this artist's bedroom a very special shade of blue has been used on the walls and in the choice of fabric for the curtains. It is warm rather than cool and gives an inviting glow to the room when lit by a small bedside lamp.*

A child's room may require many special features: open floor space for games; built-in worktops for homework and crafts; adjustable shelves; good lighting; washable, durable surfaces; sturdy beds that can survive the transition from crib to open bed; stacking bunks or trundle beds for shared rooms.

Beds for young children need firm mattresses that are lightweight and washable, such as foam blocks. Webbed slats offer a suitable, ventilated, inexpensive bed base – lightweight, too, for stacking bunks. For a baby, you can find a big cot with detachable slatted drop sides which converts into a single bed. If you start with a standard cot, upgrade to stacking bunks, since children usually enjoy having friends to stay overnight. A Continental quilt and fitted bottom sheet supply an easy-care bedding option: polyester-filled Continental quilts are washable and non-allergenic. When choosing the bed-linen and wall coverings for a child's room, resist the temptation to launch a theme bedroom that its occupant will outgrow sooner than you intend to redecorate. Parents' enthusiasm for sci-fi or cartoon characters may not be matched by the child's, so provide plain walls on which they can place their own decorations.

Walls should be finished with washable paint rather than wallpaper, since few small children can resist the temptation to peel off paper. Posters can be replaced as interests change.

Firm base flooring must be tough and smooth. Stained and sealed floorboards make a good surface for games, as does the heavy-duty cord carpet which is bathroom-rated to withstand splashes. Scratchy but durable floor coverings like jute or cork are appropriate for a teenager's bedroom.

Space is important for people of all ages: play-pens for toddlers, play areas for school-age children, work space for older ones and room for teenagers to entertain. Folding chairs stack away to clear the floor. Rather than investing in special wardrobes for children's clothes, many of which do not need to hang, find good toy and equipment storage systems which will keep toys tidy but accessible.

Learning through sight and sound is basic to this generation so do not underestimate the wiring requirements: supply enough sockets for a television (which doubles as a VDU for the home computer), a video recorder beneath the television, a music centre or stereo, a radio, a clock and any lighting required for work areas. Ensure that all wall sockets have safety shields to prevent a toy, or worse, a finger being experimentally fed in. For electronic equipment to work in harmony and look good, allow for space to house records, tapes and computer gear and a means to keep the tangle of wires under control. There are many alternatives, from purpose-built desks to trolleys for moving the television to the computer keyboard when it is needed as a Visual Display Unit.

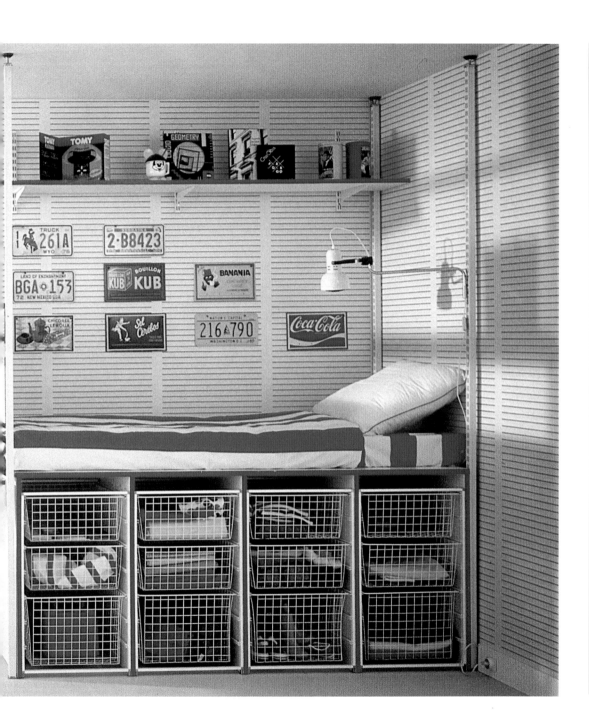

SAFETY CHECKLIST

- Enclose exposed radiator panels with fireguards.
- Never keep portable heaters or fires in a child's room.
- Use wall-mounted lights in a toddler's room.
- Shield all socket outlets with safety covers.
- Use reinforced thick panes in low-level windows.
- Remove keys from any locks on nursery doors.
- Fit a gate or barrier to restrict access to staircases.
- Select fire-retardant materials for soft furnishings and mattresses.
- Find sturdy, stable furniture without sharp edges or splinters.
- Free-standing furniture likely to topple if pushed or pulled should be bolted to the wall.
- Baby chairs or bouncers must stand on the floor, never on a tabletop.
- Fit a safety rail across an under-five-year-old's bed.
- Top bunk beds need a safety rail and a ladder bolted on.
- Any painted surfaces should be washable, durable and lead-free.

Although this bedroom is small, it appears spacious because of the wallpaper in white with fine red lines, open wire baskets and red detailing on shelf edges. The biggest single block of colour lies on the bed with broad vertical and horizontal bands of scarlet and white.

The nursery is the one room where purpose-built furniture is needed, possibly for as little as four years. So there is an advantage to be gained in buying furniture systems that are designed to make the transition from babyhood to toddler with your child, matching changes in both size and needs. The nursery has to house the crib or cot, the child-size wardrobe, pint-size desks and chairs, and toys. Storage systems must be tidy yet easily accessible to the child. Avoid furniture that topples or is too cumbersome.

1 In this spacious nursery, maximum floor space is freed for play, with sanded and sealed floorboards left plain to provide a smooth area. It is more practical for the small child who often plays on hands and knees than prickly jute or unevenly furry carpet. Blocks of foam covered in starry fabric provide alternative seating and impromptu housing, while the little yellow tubular steel chairs pull up at low-level desks. Open stacking boxes that will not topple house childish amusements against the wall, while the same shapes in deeper boxes are given a base and used for toys, to stack away at the end of the day. The same furniture system adapts from babyhood to the toddler's bedroom.

1

2

3

4

MAKING A TOY STORAGE BOX

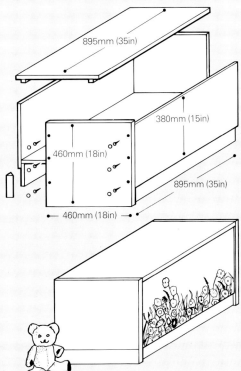

895mm (35in)

380mm (15in)

460mm (18in)

895mm (35in)

460mm (18in)

This toy chest is easy to make from panels of plywood or blockboard, or any sheet material which can be drilled and screwed. **1** Cut four side panels to the dimensions indicated in the drawing, making sure to cut them squarely. **2** Mark and drill screw holes as illustrated. **3** Glue and screw the side panels into place. Check diagonals for squareness. **4** Cut four bottom bearer pieces from a piece of wood. Glue and screw into the corners of the side panels. **5** Cut the bottom piece to fit and glue in place, resting on top of the bottom bearers. **6** Cut the lid to fit, allowing for the top edge of the side panels at each end. Mark hinge-fixing holes, drill and screw hinges into place. **7** Decorate the box with bright paint and adhesive cut-outs.

2 The cot, cupboard and small changing area above the wardrobe offer all the requirements of a nursery: a safe and protected sleep area, somewhere to store clothes behind closed doors and an open shelving system for quick access that supports a plastic-covered foam block for changing and bathing the baby. The heavy-duty flat weave cord carpet is rated suitable for bathrooms since it can withstand splashing.

3 Once the slatted sides from the drop-side cot are removed permanently, the cot becomes a bed. Without its foam top, the worktop is transformed into a practical desk, and the storage system pulls out to become a bedside table that holds the books. The stool swivels to different heights as the child grows.

4 Since the furniture in this nursery is not adaptable, it is feasible to decorate it with stick-on cartoon characters and stencils that an older child will outgrow around the same time as the furniture. Toys are tidied away into the big lidded wicker basket.

Beds take up a lot of space in the child's room where floor area is at a premium. There are many solutions, ranging from the stacking bunk bed to the platform bed above a cupboard, shelves and worktop. Stacking beds are invaluable when young children share a room, or invite friends home. But such beds need to be shelved when the child is between ten and twelve, so those that separate into two are useful.

1 *This room, shared by two brothers, will grow up with them, though they need not grow apart when the beds do. Easily changed into two singles, the bunk bed does not have a base that is too weighty. A webbing roll or wooden slats will support a light but firm foam base, covered with fitted sheets and the easy-care Continental quilt. Stacking boxes on castors for bed-linen or toys can fit underneath the bed. Here, fabric pockets pinned on the wall provide extra storage for lightweight possessions.*

2 *In this ship-shape bedroom, the platform sleeping area is reached by a ladder built into a structural wooden frame with muslin drapes like sails above. The modular unit comprises storage shelves with sliding doors like those in a ship's cabin. Lights are suspended on chains, alongside a yacht.*

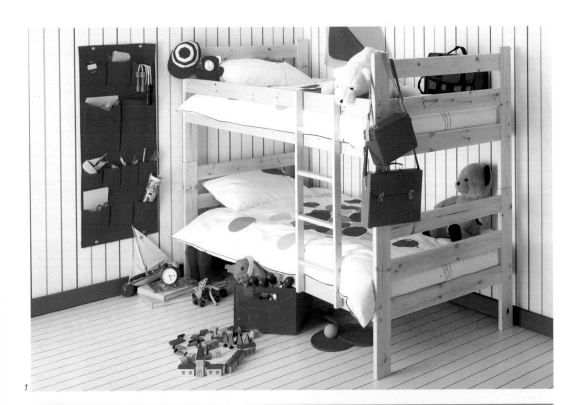

1

2

3

4

5

3 This custom-built stacked bed offers space below for a worktop area, with cupboard and bookshelves, and a ladder. Children's cupboards can waste space since their clothes are much smaller and hanging rails should be set lower than usual.

4 A shared room that allows for differing interests, from tennis and skiing to skate-boarding and model-building, even goldfish-minding. With so many divergent interests, lots of work and storage space is essential. It has to be adaptable. The pine shelving system has adjustable pegs to support shelves at differing heights. The addition of a laminated top makes a simple but workmanlike desk. Jute flooring at this stage in a child's development is fine since it offers a practical, hard-wearing surface at a stage when the occupants have stopped playing on their knees and need worktops and shelving.

5 The children who share this playroom have separated a stacking bunk bed into two sofabeds – the peg top at each corner of the bed reveals its origins. A fitted base sheet and patterned cushions like bolsters make these beds into daytime sofas for listening to music and talking to friends, while bulky Continental quilts are stacked in the centrally placed blue blanket box.

As the child moves towards his teens, basic furniture and furnishings need to allow for individuality. Now the child's personality can be imprinted upon the space, and personal tastes are reflected in the possessions. These are rooms for single occupancy – no longer shared with siblings.

1 An attic bedroom has a treasury of portraits, both photographic and painted, even postcards, framed and hung like a Victorian collection. An old washstand is given a fake marble top of adhesive paper. Other theatrical touches include the embroidered shawl draped over the bentwood chair, the collection of film star pictures, a ceramic bust and a dressmaker's model. The cast-iron brass bed dressed with a plain white antique lace and crochet cover and old crochet pillow slips gives this room an 'olde worlde' charm.

2 This splendid iron bed has enclosed sides to stop the small child from falling out. Now the occupant is older, that safety frame painted blue becomes a trellised frame for soft toys. In the small alcove behind the bed an unusual collection of costumed dolls of many nations gains importance. So a simple space, as small as a child's bed, doubles up by day as a display case for the child's interests and hobbies.

1

2

3

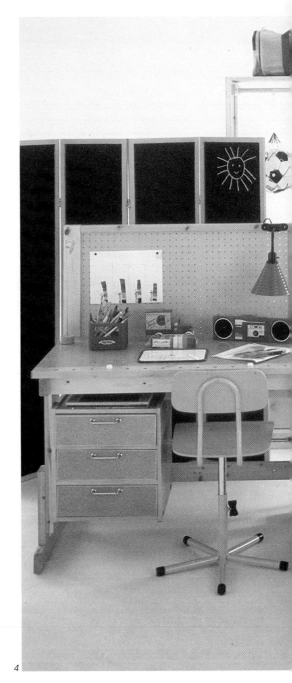

4

SUPPORT SYSTEMS FOR SHELVES

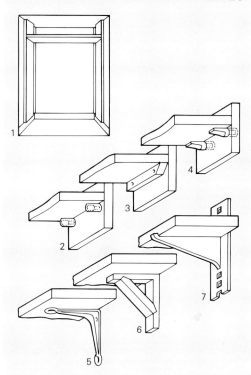

1 Strips of wood 12-18mm (½-¾in) thick fixed to the walls can support short shelving systems. Shelves are supported at each end. **2** Holes can be drilled into upright wooden standards for metal or plastic dowels which act as shelf end supports. **3** Narrow 25mm (1in) battens screwed into upright standards also act as shelf end supports. **4** Long plastic- or rubber-sleeved screws make decorative end supports for glass shelves, which are particularly effective for displaying houseplants in window bays. **5** Pressed steel brackets are strong enough to support heavy weights when used along the length of a shelf, rather than at the ends. **6** Home-made triangular wooden brackets are suitable for areas such as sheds or garages. **7** Wall-mounted bars with special slot-in brackets form a flexible, adjustable shelving system (see page 31 for installation instructions).

3 New angles on a bedroom where even the wall surfaces are banded geometrically in eau-de-Nil *upon white, delineated with a border. Broad bands of these colours are used in the bedspread. The outline of the simple white modern bed is softened with a very tall drape, simple to attach to a coronet or ring fixed to the wall, with the fabric stapled round it. A specially designed corner storage unit takes full advantage of double display windows to house a collection of toys.*

4 Bridging the gap between childhood and teens is a furniture system that is flexible, neither too babyish nor too grown up. Here are some basics which can adapt to individual tastes and spaces. A simple wooden desk that can be tilted to become a draughtsman's slanted worktop has a pegboard back to the desktop on which work can be posted and which stops pencils and books from falling off if the desk is not placed against a wall. A screen that is also a blackboard provides a foldaway partition for a work area; a painted trunk offers storage space for clothes; bins house games and artists' materials. Simple wooden poles, fitted with pegs that adjust, hold shelves at varying heights as well as wardrobe rails and drawers.

*1 Until now, platform beds
featured in children's rooms
have been adventure
playgrounds reached by rope
ladders and rigging. Now, the
platform bed in a teenager's
bedroom uses stacking boxes
at the right height for records
and books as a base for an
informal bed. The mattress is
covered in a zany colourful
print, with solid colour
cushions scattered upon it to
form the backrest. Black
framed prints propped against
the wall, and two simple tables
with solid acrylic tops, in
primary colours, provide
practical surfaces. The little
slanted bedside lamp uses a
low-voltage halogen bulb to
give an intense beam of light
for bedside reading.*

*2 A bed frame of tubular chrome
clamps together in various
combinations. Here, a bed
raised upon a platform base
has the bed area delineated
above with a netting top while
the clamped side sections
form a desktop for the screen
and computer keyboard. A
scarlet tractor-seat stool
provides simple seating. The
only other item of furniture is
the black lacquer trolley which
can bring a TV screen nearer
the keyboard, or house the
video. Bed lighting is provided
by spotlights which clamp on
to the tubular frame.*

1

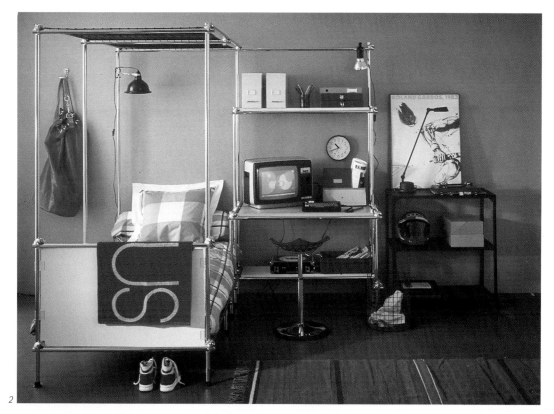

3 The privacy of an alcove retreat is achieved very simply with wooden battens fixed to the ceiling to which curtains are stapled. The room, painted pale yellow to that point, becomes a peaceful pale grey in the alcove. The bedding is an ikat flat-weave quilted counterpane which determines the colours for the pink, green and blue cushions. Beyond the screen, the work area is delineated by a roll-top desk. The work table slides back to be concealed beneath the top. An angled floor lamp throws light where it is needed most.

4 Just as the last room was a peaceful retreat, this room is a vigorous, imaginative area. At the base is a bed, above it another floor, the awning shielding the playhouse area. Within the basic framework there is endless opportunity for imagination; areas can become a crow's nest aboard a ship, look-out posts, or camps. More practically, within the framework is incorporated a rail for clothes – and Kermit the frog.

Wall-mounted or surface-mounted lights are recommended for children's bedrooms since lights are easily knocked over in pillow fights or any rumbustious activity. But the new low-voltage lights set into lightweight plastic fittings can withstand knocks without shocks. They are fun as well as functional. Many of them can be left on all night in rooms where children are unsure about sleeping in the dark. Adequate lighting at worktop areas should be provided from special clamp-on lamps that alter position as required, since young eyes are easily strained. In teenagers' bedrooms you will need lots of socket outlets for hair driers, record players, computers and televisions.

1 *Balloons tethered to the wall: their strings are the leads which link the low-voltage bulbs with the socket outlet.*

2 *Small children's favourite, the windmill, in a simple paper shade that conceals a small bulb. The lead is concealed in the stick-like lamp base.*

3 *Lights encased in durable plastic trainer shoes are low voltage so it matters little if they topple over as here, in this studied set piece.*

4 *A paper bag filled with toy cut-outs becomes a 'carry home' night light for small children.*

1

2

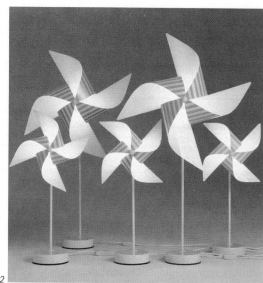

3

4

5

6

7

8

Windows often enable a desk to take advantage of natural daylight and window treatments should take note of this.

5 *A skylight in an attic bedroom painted scarlet has a smart red worktop built underneath. Venetian blinds screen it.*

6 *More scarlet frames, this time at a modern window where the printed fabric is stiffened with a roller blind kit, set simply at the window. With such a bold children's print, it is worth keeping the window treatment simple.*

7 *Trompe-l'oeil wall paintings in a children's room can look marvellous. But often the child wearies of the scene, or outgrows the parents' enthusiasm for Mickey Mouse or space-age fantasies. A simpler way to inject individualism into a room, as well as mask a tiresome inner-city view of buildings, is to paint a roller blind. Or, as here, use metallic paint in high gloss upon Venetian blinds.*

8 *A novel idea is to dress the window with muslin drapes pleated at the heading and attached by painted pegs to a flattened batten. The desk on crayon legs, designed by Frenchman Pierre Sala, has a lift-up laminated top attached by spiral ring-binder clips, with a drawing pad as its base.*

BATHROOMS

More than any other room, the bathroom is the place to pamper yourself, even though warm, pleasurable bathrooms often must be planned in tiny spaces. It is the skimpiest room in the modern house; the average bathroom built today measures just 1.5m × 2m (5ft × 7ft). A standard 1.5m (5ft) bath fits snugly along one wall and is usually 76cm (2½ft) wide, effectively squeezing the basin and toilet into the remaining 1.37m (4½ft) of the abutting wall. Planning a bathroom in a space the size of a closet is a real challenge.

There is limited scope for individuality in bathroom design since the room contains the least flexible of all household items – the bath, basin and toilet, rigid objects which conform to a basic shape. Interior designers and architects relieve this uniformity in many ways, often by introducing different surface finishes, such as plain or patterned ceramic tiles, various paint finishes, tongue-and-groove wood panelling, laminates, mirrors, marble, plastics and many more.

If you are planning a completely new bathroom you have far more opportunity than if you are redecorating an existing one. A visit to bathroom dealers' showrooms, where baths, basins, toilets and other fittings are displayed in room sets, will help you envisage the impact of the various styles available. Consider them in relation to your bathroom: will a boldly coloured suite make your space look smaller? Will ultra-modern fittings blend well in an older building?

With the measurements and specifications of the fittings you like, work out how you can place them in your bathroom. The lay-out must follow basic plumbing and electrical wiring considerations, so seek expert advice as soon as possible. Allow for safety and comfort when placing the fittings, and check that the floor will support the weight of heavy fittings, such as old-fashioned cast-iron bath tubs.

Just because the bathroom is the smallest room in the house there is no need for it to be the dullest. Patterned and coloured surfaces will bring the room to life. Adding a co-ordinated range of bathroom accessories – soap dish, toothbrush holder, cupholder, shelf, medicine cabinet, toilet-roll holder, framed mirror, towel rail, wastepaper basket, laundry basket – can brighten and unify an existing bathroom. Remember too that bathroom linens – towels, face cloths and shower curtains – can be used to great effect.

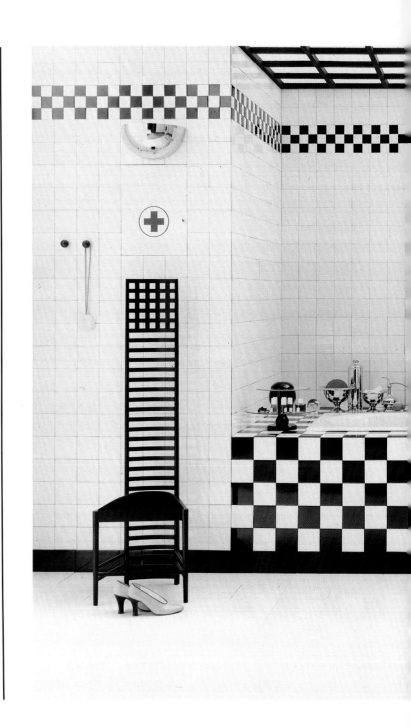

PLANNING CHECKLIST

- How many people use the bathroom?
- Are any users young or elderly?
  Provide non-slip surfaces, easy access to lights and mirrors, hand-grip baths.
- Do you have room for a full bath?
  If not, consider a corner bath, deep-soak tub or shower.
- Will the shower head be at least 1m (3¼ft) below the water tank base?
  If not, install a pump.
- Is it necessary to move the toilet?
  Re-site it as close as possible to existing soil pipes to save money.
- Do you want to install a bidet?
  It is cheaper to install an over-rim bidet than a rim supply model.
- Are shaver sockets out of reach from the bath?
- Is there good general, as well as directional, light?
- Are light fixtures operated by either a pullcord switch or a remote switch next to the door?
- Is the bathroom overcrowded?
  Relieve the pressure by adding:
  - separate toilet
  - bedroom
  - alcove shower
  - wash basin

Bold bathrooms need not be expensively fitted. This dramatic chequerboard pattern is easy to reproduce with cheap tiles. Use graph paper to pace out the measurements and changes in pattern, and work from the centre outwards.

1 A porcelain roll-top bath left free-standing, like an old-fashioned hot tub, next to an elegant basin. These traditional fittings, reproduced today, do not attempt to conceal the plumbing, so the pipes that lead to the taps are often left on view. In this plain white bathroom, central wall-mounted taps with concealed plumbing give an uncluttered effect. Elegant chromed legs support a wall-mounted basin with fine chromed towel rails at each side. The clean lines of the contemporary fittings – wall mirror above the basin, shaving mirror clamped to the bath and small table with perspex surround – distinguish the background. The narrow blue edge bordering the large wall tiles and bonsai tree provide splashes of colour and points of interest in an otherwise bare background which offsets the strong shapes of the basin and bath.

1

FITTING A BATH PANEL

Traditional baths made from enamelled cast iron are undoubtedly durable and handsome, but the high cost and weight of cast iron make it an impractical choice for most bathrooms. Modern baths made from a variety of materials, usually either moulded acrylic sheet or cast perspex sheeting reinforced with glass fibre with a vitreous enamel finish, are lightweight, chip-proof and, because they retain heat, energy-saving. The matching side panels supplied with many baths are intended to fit the maximum installed size, but these can easily be cut to fit the height of the bath as installed.

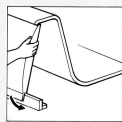

1 Fix a 12mm (½in) plinth within a line drawn on the floor below the bath rim.

2 Fit edge of panel under lip of bath, noting where it contacts the plinth.

2

2 A more luxurious treatment for the same small bathroom is to have it entirely panelled with a practical spatter-effect laminate. It creates a blue haze attractive for contrasting contemporary fittings: a very plain white rectangular bath and elaborate burnished chrome basin both boxed in the same laminate. A heater tubular steel towel rail and a small glass-topped table look good with the 1930s-style metal fittings for taps, soap, splashbacks and basin. The laminate is used to make a recessed panel behind the bath and a fitted unit which provides useful shelving for storage of towels and bottles under the basin.

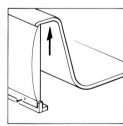
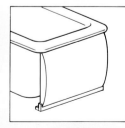

3 If the panel is too long, trim a section from the wall end.

4 Push panel edge firmly under bath lip and screw bottom edge to plinth.

5 Place end panels in position before front panels using same method.

6 Fit panels to baths with timber frames by fixing plinth to bottom batten.

Space planning in bathrooms needs careful consideration: they are statistically the smallest room in the house, yet contain certain bulky fittings which, when plumbed in, become fixtures. There are certain essentials which cannot be altered and must be taken into consideration before planning starts: the bulky shapes of the ceramic ware and a water source with adequate inlet pressure and outlet drainage. The bath is the first consideration since it is so bulky. Corner baths free floor space, as do rectangular baths set flush against a wall. A freestanding bath, on the other hand, can be used to partition space. In a tiny bathroom, the easiest solution is to line up the sanitary ware against the outside wall. Various combinations are offered here. By the time a full-size bath tub shower, basin, toilet and bidet have been installed, even the best-planned bathroom can begin to seem cluttered. Choose one of the lighter shades of sanitary ware if the room is small, to create an illusion of space, and consider matching wall and floor tiles.

THE COMPACT BATHROOM

This compact bathroom is designed to be built into a walk-in cupboard, although the plan would do as well for an impossibly tiny bathroom. Within a meagre 1830mm × 1830mm (6ft × 6ft) space, all the basic products are plumbed in, and an allowance is made for the opening of the bathroom door, which cuts a 915mm (3ft) swathe through the room.

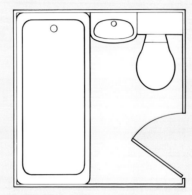

This space-saving bathroom contains everything required in a 2285mm × 2285mm (7½ft × 7½ft) room. A shower over the bath cuts hot water consumption – an important consideration in these days of energy conservation – and the bidet is sited in the best possible place, next to the toilet, for ease of use.

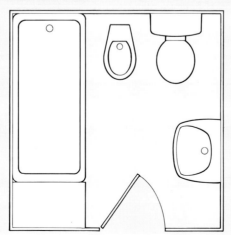

ROOM FOR IMPROVEMENT

BEFORE
A large bathroom is wasted when everyone squabbles over who is to use it first.

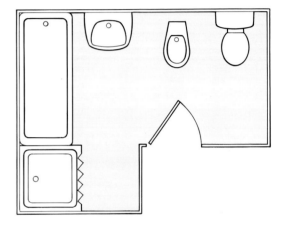

BEFORE
It can make good sense to combine separate facilities in one room.

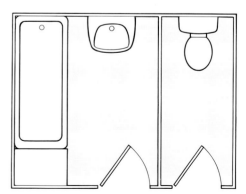

AFTER

A bathroom which contains the sole household toilet is far from ideal. If there is no space or budget allowance to add a second bathroom, dividing a large bathroom with a partition wall into two separate areas can be the best solution. In this conversion, one room is reserved for bathing and the other self-contained room houses a toilet, bidet and small hand basin. The original room had two windows, but when dividing a room with one window, remember to allow for adequate ventilation.

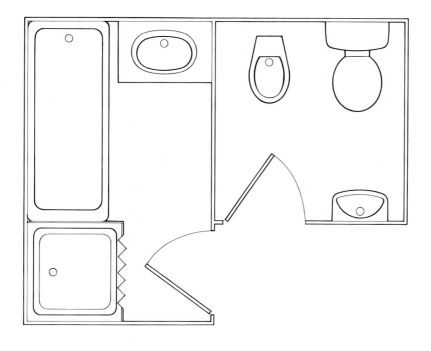

AFTER

Removing a wall and a door has opened out this bathroom. Without moving the toilet there is now room for a double 'his and hers' wash basin to cope with the morning rush, and space for the bidet. This solution is not recommended for the large, one-toilet household. For a small family, however, or in a home with a second toilet, combining the spartan toilet and the separate bathroom creates a large, luxurious room. Now there is room for another product, whether a bidet or a shower, or even a comfortable easy chair.

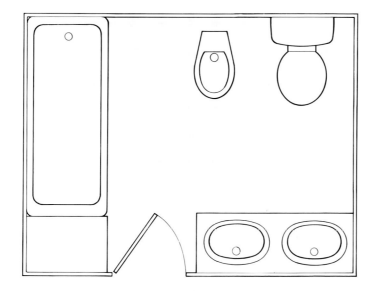

When you have managed to squeeze the essentials into your existing bathroom, whether large or small, it is not uncommon to find that no additional amenities can get around the perennial problem of morning-time congestion when there is only one bathroom to serve a large family. Take a good look round the house, remembering that a toilet or a shower occupies very little space. If a cupboard under the stairs serves as a refuge for outdoor clothing or cleaning equipment, perhaps the space could be put to better use as a mini-shower room complete with toilet and small wash basin, as illustrated below. Such a conversion would require special plumbing, but the expense and trouble could be well worth it. A windowless bathroom created underneath a staircase or in a closet should be ventilated by a fan which comes on automatically.

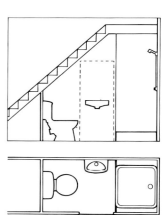

Your choice of bath needs careful consideration to fit the space since it is the bulkiest fixture. If the bathroom already installed is not to your taste, either in colour or shape, consider decorative treatments around the bath.

1 *Corner baths can wedge neatly into a room. Here, an awkwardly shaped semi-circular bay has a corner bath – and a modern, sculptural slim-line basin. The triptych mirror with arched tops is similarly geometric in its angles and curves, centrally placed for display. Slabs of white marble – reproduced in look-alike Corian – give this elegant bathroom its luxurious finish.*

2 *Whatever it is called – 'Champagne', 'Savannah' or 'Pampas' – the beige bath is anonymous. It is more difficult to use since it lacks individuality. Plain white goods are easier; so, too, are the more emphatic colours. Here the bath is given distinction by the white glossy surface surrounds and Art Deco styling, always outlined in black, with the mirror and palms and sandalwood boxes.*

3 *A free-standing roll-top cast-iron tub, placed centrally in a room, makes a feature of the plumbing. The pipes are brass and the six graphic paintings are all framed in brass.*

1

2

3

BASIC BATHS

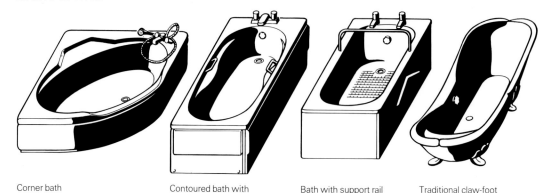

Corner bath

Contoured bath with hand grips

Bath with support rail and grip base

Traditional claw-foot bath

4

5

6

FITTING A SHOWER SCREEN

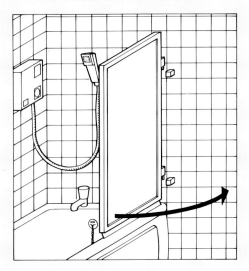

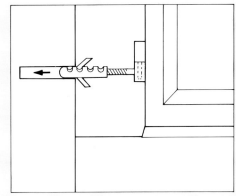

1 Position the screen on the top rim of the bath. Ensure that it is held vertically and that the bottom flipper makes an adequate seal on the bath edge. **2** Mark the position of the hinges on the wall, drill holes with a 7mm (¼in) bit, making the hole deeper than the plug. **3** Fit the plug into the wall and screw the cup into the plug. **4** Drop the screen into position. **5** To align the bottom flipper with the bath rim, simply adjust the cups.

4 Here, a centrally placed bath in a large room acts as a partition between bedroom and dressing room. Curtains on rods suspended from the ceiling close off the area, providing privacy for this unusual lay-out and creating an impromptu bathroom.

5 Striped lavender wallpaper visually extends the height of this small bathroom, while the horizontal stripes of louvred shutters appear to widen what is, in fact, the narrowest wall. The bath is similarly deceptive, creating more space than a block of solid colour would, though the basin is grey. Even the space in the corner is used with a wicker storage unit housing mementoes of seaside holidays.

6 This panelled bath disguises the workings of a whirlpool bath with controls that vary the intensity of the water jets. Sloping walls of the attic bathroom are useful in the bath area where the occupant need never stand up, while the shower section moves forward into the room for greater height. The boxed-in partition wall at the back creates a small step-in shower behind glass doors.

Planners recommend installing a built-in pump to boost water pressure. With the right rose and a booster pump aerating the water, it can feel as luxurious as if you were showering with champagne.

1   *Here, a round deep tub is reached by a tiered platform, tiled in white. The basin has the same lines. At the foot of the hot tub, a shower cubicle is glassed in behind doors. In this confined area, the use of tiles, mirrors and glass creates an impression of spaciousness.*

2   *The central triangular pillar houses the water pipes and booster pump for this shower. Variations in floor level height are minimized by the use of narrow tiles, varying in scale from the wall tiles. Both the round mirror and the bulkhead light give a ship-shape finish to the bathroom.*

3   *This tailor-made shower cubicle is added to the base of a panelled bath which is set on a long wall. Tongue-and-groove panelling with a matt varnish finish increases the sauna feeling, as does the step up into the shower above the skirting. You can build your own cubicle around a shower tray or buy pre-fabricated cubicles complete with tray, back panel, sides and doors.*

1

SHOWER TRAYS AND HEADS

Shower trays   Sliding and pivoting shower heads   Edwardian bath mixer

3

4

5

4   *A cast-iron roll-top bath becomes a walk-in hot tub, evoking a Japanese interior with its wooden platform leading simply to the central tub. Pipes and taps set in the wooden panelling like a screen against the wall add to this illusion. At the window is a tatami grass reed woven blind, much wider than the window.*

5   *An alternative shower fitted above a bath has been created by boxing in an area in the awkwardly shaped bay with low partition walls, which house the taps and inlet water pipes. This type of shower uses water directly from the mains, which is heated by a small instant heater fitted close to the shower behind the tiled panel. As the water temperature increases, the shower water pressure may decrease.*

MAKING A SUNKEN BATH

Steps leading to a raised and tiled area around the tub create the impression of a simple sunken bath. A bath filled with water and a person is very heavy, so place boards beneath levelling feet to spread the load over the floorboards.

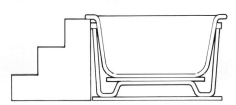

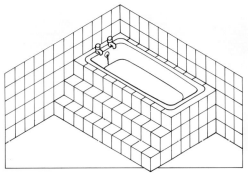

Toilets need to be set against the outer wall for access to soil waste. Modern toilets are usually made with one of two sorts of flushing mechanisms: wash-down or syphonic systems, both found in many styles. This cistern may fit to the back of the bowl without any visible connection, or may be hidden, along with the pipes in ducted units, behind removable panels or wall-hung systems.

1 This wall-hung toilet has a steel cistern set above like a wall safe of burnished steel. Concealed ducts are hidden in the tiled wall. This syphonic model is quieter than the flushing mechanism of the wash-down toilet.

2 Neater, more stylish, this close-coupled toilet is a favourite for modern apartments. It features a cistern that fits directly to the back of the bowl without any connecting pipe. Here, the room achieves an Oriental simplicity with parchment blinds outlined in charcoal.

1

2

3

TOILETS AND BIDETS

Syphonic close-coupled toilet | Toilet with low-level cistern | Wash-down toilet | Silent-flushing toilet without cistern | Wall-hung toilet | Bidet with separate taps | Bidet with over-rim mixer tap

4

3   The least expensive, wash-down, plain white sanitary ware is elevated by more expensive fittings – the platform floor that raises this section of the bathroom and the low-level shelving. It acts as a storage system as well as shielding this area.

4   This back-to-the-wall toilet cistern with matching bidet is separated by a low-level wall structured to screen only at sitting height. On most bidet models you sit facing the wall, so there should be enough room for knees. Some bidets are fitted with an ascending spray in their base: bidet mixer taps may also incorporate a spray. This model has wall-mounted taps, surely an encouragement to face the right way. Water comes into a bidet either through over-rim supply from basin-like taps, or heated rim mixer taps which control the temperature of the water coming into the fitting from the rim.

INSTALLING A BIDET

Over-rim bidets are plumbed in exactly the same way as wash basins. In most cases, this means branching off pipes which supply other bathroom equipment. Always ensure that the position of the bidet allows plenty of room at the back for properly connecting the waste pipe. If possible, site it next to a toilet. Before fixing the bidet, do as much plumbing as possible. Connect the waste pipe to a hopper or soil stack. Fix the taps, which can be two single taps or a 100mm (4in) basin mixer tap. Finally, secure the bidet to the floor using carefully tightened brass screws.

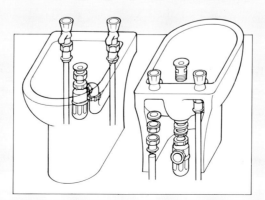

Basins come in many shapes and sizes. The two standard sizes are 455mm × 635mm (18in × 28in) and 405mm × 560mm (16in × 22in), while the shapes are oval, rectangular, square or circular. There are three main types of basin: pedestal, wall-hung and built-in. The base for a basin built into a countertop, which can be a standard self-assembly or custom-built unit, always provides storage. Variations on these three main types are illustrated here.

1 Wall-hung basins are usually set at a height of 815mm (32in) from floor to rim, though this height can vary. The basin is usually provided with an additional means of support, as here. A cross bar between supports provides a useful towel rail.

2 The pedestal basin has a central support stem which partly conceals plumbing. Here, the ceramic detailing suggests an earlier age, as does the shaped ceramic splashback that is a part of the basin top. Accessories are in mahogany and brass with cross-head taps to keep to the turn-of-the-century theme.

1

2

BASIC WASH BASINS

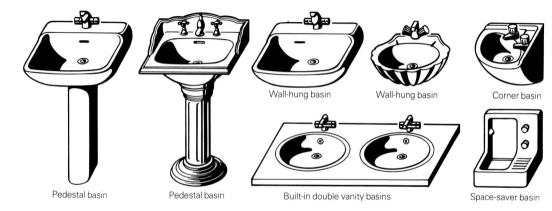

Pedestal basin

Pedestal basin

Wall-hung basin

Wall-hung basin

Corner basin

Built-in double vanity basins

Space-saver basin

3

4

5

6

TAPS AND ACCESSORIES

Basin mixer tap

Basin pillar taps

Basin mixer tap with fixed spout

Basin mixer tap with
swivel spout

Accessory set in plastic-coated wire

Cup and toothbrush holder

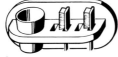

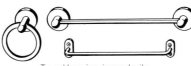

Towel-hanging ring and rails

3 A slimline hand basin, too small for hair-washing, is ideal for this tiny bathroom planned in a cupboard. Shower mixer heads added to the bath bring a shower as well to this area.

4 In a long, narrow bathroom a double basin housed in a custom-built worktop breaks up the corridor-like space. The basin backdrop is the narrow line-up of vertical panes of glass. A tangle of creepers provides privacy without any window cover.

5 An oval hand basin set into a black tiled worktop has its shape emphasized dramatically. Fine striped muslin curtains cut short to worktop height frame the window which is painted lavender. Attention to detail is important with this sophisticated colour mix of lavender, black and white: even the irises match.

6 An oval basin with its own white splashtop area is set into a purpose-built worktop tiled in terracotta ceramic tiles and with storage shelves below. The arrangement of mirrors and storage shelves has been designed to make the most of the asymmetrical placement of the basin on the worktop.

Mirrors are essential in any bathroom since the very nature of the room involves shaving, washing, putting on make-up. Most often placed above the basin, mirrors can be found in less likely places as well – beside the bath or lining an entire wall to give the illusion of more space. For large areas of mirror, you need a solid wall, rather than a flimsy partition. Mirrors need to be well lit. Good lighting makes your bathroom more attractive, pleasant and safe to use. Options include wall-mounted surface fittings, the popular bulkhead light, recessed downlighters and diffused fluorescent lighting usually found in battens installed above the mirror or bathroom medicine chest. Whilst it is not the most flattering light, it lasts the longest. Remember, extra light is needed on the front and sides of the mirrors.

1 In practical rooms like bathrooms there is rarely space for any idiosyncrasies to be highlighted. Yet the owner of this bathroom has fixed a mirror to the wall at the right height for shaving while seated in the bath. Centrally placed taps make this feasible. Some other highly individual possessions are housed in this unconventional little bathroom.

1

2

3

4

FITTING MIRROR TILES

1 Wall surface must be clean, dry and free from flaking paint. Divide wall into quarters by drawing a vertical and a horizontal line across centre. **2** Remove protective wax paper from one side of four pieces of mounting tape and stick them on each corner of the back of a mirror tile about 12mm (½in) from the edge. Press firmly. Remove remaining wax paper and mount the first tile at centre of area where two lines intersect. **3** Work outwards in a horizontal row, filling each quarter section until only tiles which need to be cut remain. **4** Measure distance to be filled and mark measurement on mirror side of a tile. Place on a firm surface and score with a glass cutter. Break in two, then mount as before.

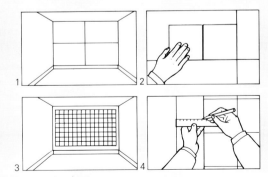

2 *A more conventional treatment is a long mirror edged with a specially designed light fitting above it, like an actor's dressing room mirror. Light is important in this small space – even the windows are not covered but left bare with frosted glass.*

3 *Mirrored panels across the cupboard doors double the images of this tiny bathroom with its white panelled bath, pedestal basin, and special fitment for the bathroom mirror. Yellow striped wallpaper creates an illusory height in the room, and the bold blue and white striped director's chair fits neatly beside the bath for the bathtime supervision of the rubber dinghy launch.*

4 *Navy tiles form a nautical line-up above the red louvred doors of this wash basin unit. Above it the pin board has clips to hold toothmugs and other items. The mirrored panel is lit with a red bulkhead light. Trolleys provide useful trundle-around storage and this scarlet, epoxy-coated wire trolley suits the red, white and blue theme of the bathroom.*

Just because bathroom surfaces have to be tough, waterproof and easy to clean, there is no need to keep them workmanlike. Theatrical backgrounds can be created with tiles, mirrors, paints and borders, as you can discover in the bathrooms illustrated here.

Certainly, in the steamy atmosphere of the bathroom, moisture-proof wall coverings are essential. Coated washable papers or sheeny water-resistant paints are best. Glossy paint shows marks upon its shiny glazed surface, which is fine for small surface detailing, but not so good over large areas.

The new marble look-alike, Corian, is light, durable, easy to batten to the wall and more fashionable than the tongue-and-groove panel boards reminiscent of Scandinavian saunas. Hardwood panels, boarding and marble slabs all share a great advantage, despite their discrepancies in cost and application – they hide the pipes. So do wall units in the fitted bathroom.

Shower walls should be tiled, with a grooved, non-slip floor area. Perspex, shatter-proof glass, tiles or plastic laminate boards can be used to panel the shower.

Ceramic tiles are always popular. Colourful patterned tiles now available can re-create any backdrop, such as an Islamic carpet, a seaside scene or a flowery glade. Floor tiles can be cold in winter, so only use them, with accessible walkways, in a warm bathroom. Water-resistant flooring, like cushioned vinyl, is not slippery. Continuous sheet flooring is more difficult to lay than vinyl tiles in an awkward or irregular space, but the joints between tiles can admit moisture and tiles lift more easily over a duration of time. Cork and duckboard are popular surface finishes for tiles – untreated cork is better than polyurethane-sealed cork. Plastic laminate boards one metre square have become a fashion flooring, despite their cost, since they can reproduce on a smaller scale the dazzling patterns of grand Italian terrazzos, copied from the squares and churches in Rome and Venice. To unify a small space, employ these patterns boldly and use the same surface pattern to cover the bath panels.

If you want to tackle a painted duckboard floor, paint sanded sheets of duckboard with yachting shipdeck paints, seeking inspiration for your design from earlier examples, such as the floor at the Victoria and Albert Museum in London, or the stencilled floorboards of the American Museum in Bath. Begin at the borders to anchor your pattern and set you on the right scale.

Windows can be screened with etched, opaque or stained glass. Stick on your own coloured cellophane paper for mock stained glass – there are kits that reproduce some dazzling patterns from baroque houses and Gothic churches. Consider removing the window panes and replacing them with mirror tiles, which will provide twenty-four-hour privacy and the illusion of space.

The longtime favourites for bathroom surfaces, ceramic tiles, are durable, scrubbable and good-looking. Cushioned vinyl sheeting or tiles now imitate some of the specialized surfaces that once only ceramics could produce. Other options include marble, marble look-alikes such as Corian, and wood, with choice limited to materials resistant to damp and moisture. Today, marble, terracotta or glazed surfaces may look like the real thing, but are cushioned for softness and warmth. Here, plain white tiles in two sizes are teamed with black tiles to create a stylish interior. The chequerboard effect is echoed by the towels. Plan your own scheme in two-tone tiles, plotting out the effect first on graph paper. The tiles may be set on points in a diamond pattern, or used in border patterns round the mirrors, as shown on the following pages.

Spectacular effects can be created with a mosaic of tiles, mixing patterns and colours. Or you can finish off plain tiles with a coloured grout to outline each one in a finely detailed colour that matches or contrasts. Expensive patterned tiles can be used as small details, either as a splashback or as a border edging an area of white tiles.

1 *Post-modern pastels in pink, peppermint and citrus yellow are lined up for bold contrasting candy stripes that emphasize various angles in this bathroom. Even the accessories like soap dishes and nail brushes are chosen to match and great attention is given to lighting. A large mirror set above the basin and a gloss paint on the ceiling bounces back light from myriad small starlight downlighters.*

2 *At the turn of the century, elaborately patterned tiles that evoked Islamic designs were reproduced by the Victorians. Collectors' items today, they can enliven a small base wall at the foot of a plain white bath or be used to form a splashback, as here. The bath is panelled with stained plywood decorated with mouldings and a simple lace curtain screens the area. The colours of cream and ivory with sepia are used round the room.*

1

FIXING CERAMIC TILES

Ceramic tiles are a good choice for bathrooms, where their tough, easy-to-clean and long-lasting surface is both practical and decorative. As with mirror tiles, it is best to begin by measuring the area to be tiled and calculating the number of tiles needed. Successful tiling requires careful planning. Ceramic tiles can be used for almost any bathroom surface – walls, shower compartments, countertops, ceilings and floors – but special considerations apply to using them on bathroom floors. Extra work, and thus extra expense, is likely to be necessary when laying ceramic tiles on a suspended wooden floor. Glazed ceramic tiles are slippery when wet, although unglazed tiles would be suitable for a country-style interior.

1 Fix a horizontal batten at the height of one tile above the lowest point.

2 Use a strip of wood marked off in.tile lengths to mark the batten.

2

4

3

5

3 Tiles need not be laid in regular blocks, square upon square, but may be used in a variety of ways. Here, they are tilted up in diamond-shaped patterns, creating a vigorous trellis of pale blue until the plain white border introduces a frame to the scheme. Art Nouveau detailing forms a painted border to the mirror. Fine blinds at the window keep to the same simplicity, as does the globe light above the vanity mirror.

4 Here a dramatic use of Victorian tiles encloses a bath which is divided from the bathroom by a partition. This enables the end of the bath to double as a shower, with the showerhead (not shown) fitted into the wall.

5 In the all-white bathroom, or any monochrome room, surface interest is created with texture. Here, the bevelled edge of white tiles inset along bath panels and on walls above the plain white area creates visual interest. Eau-de-Nil painted window frames and glossy cream paint create a period effect, as do the pictures engraved like old etchings and the plain wooden towel rails.

3 Fix an upright batten, using a spirit level to get a true vertical.

4 Apply 0.8 sq m (1 sq ft) of adhesive, ridging it with a notched spreader.

5 Lay tiles in horizontal lines starting from the intersection of battens.

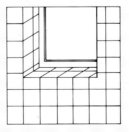

6 Cut tiles should fill odd spaces at the end of walls and ledges.

Bathroom surfaces must be waterproof, especially the floor. Linoleum is the cheapest practical flooring, with ever-popular cork tiles a close contender. Cushioned vinyl tiles, rubber-stud industrial flooring and ceramic tiles are more expensive alternatives.

1 *Tiles with fine graph-paper patterns permit accurate placement of every product and accessory in this bathroom, as well as giving a neatly squared-off precision to the finish. The floor is tiled in dappled vinyl. Mirrored walls, the clear glass-domed shower screen and opaque glass squares panelled in the partition all visually extend the actual space.*

2 *Cork tiles on the floor and the sides of the panelled bath give a warm glow to this bathroom. The coated spongeable vinyl paper has a small repeat pattern of birds on the wing.*

3 *Thatch is an unusual choice for a wall surface, yet outside a thatched wall of climbing plants, green in summer and densely vined in winter, provides an impenetrable screen to the shower. White tiles grouted in grey mix with the modern shapes and pale grey ceramics of the basin and shower tray. They bring distinctive elegance to this restrained, unusual bathroom.*

1

2

3

TILES

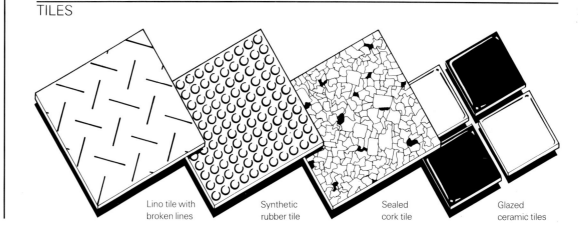

Lino tile with broken lines

Synthetic rubber tile

Sealed cork tile

Glazed ceramic tiles

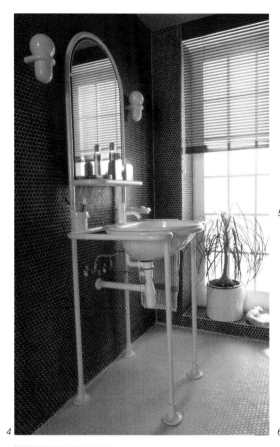

4

5

6

SHEET VINYL

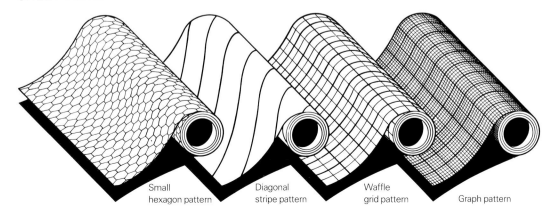

Small
hexagon pattern

Diagonal
stripe pattern

Waffle
grid pattern

Graph pattern

4 *Honeycomb-patterned flooring in white appears to push out the boundaries of this small bathroom. With such an emphatic textured floor, changing the wall surface would distance it, so the same surface finish is taken up on the walls in reverse colours of charcoal outlined with white.*

5 *This linoleum flooring imitates square tiles laid in a diamond pattern. In a bathroom where you have to cut round basin and toilet bases, it is often easiest to use vinyl sheet flooring. Here the blue and white pattern visually extends the eye to the bath panelled in glossy white ceramic tiles and the matt-finish painted wall.*

6 *This bathroom is designed to show that pattern can work effectively to extend small spaces in appearance: an elegant duo-tone reduces the impact of too many colours, while the use of small-scale patterns reduces the dramatic effect of a grand overall pattern which would visually box in the bathroom. This mosaic of tiny tiles is in reality vinyl sheeting. The walls are tiled in wheaten yellow and the entrance left a silken grey without any distracting detailing outlined in separate colour.*

Warmth is essential in the bathroom, but since electricity and water do not mix, portable electric heaters cannot be considered. Built-in electric heaters placed out of reach and operated by a pull cord are often used, and another effective solution is to have radiators or other systems linked to the heating circuit for the whole house or apartment.

1 *A heated chrome towel rail which is part of the central heating system looks extremely attractive in this bathroom. The room has a strong style and Victorian atmosphere – double basins set in marble with simple, modern mixer taps; an ornate Victorian mirror; and bare floorboards echoed by the natural wood in the cupboard doors and the stripped window frame with its floral-patterned fabric blind. Since the heated towel rail takes up space where a normal radiator could have been placed, a clever solution for heating has been found in using a slimline skirting board radiator beneath the pine vanity unit. It is effective but discreet.*

1

BATHROOM SAFETY

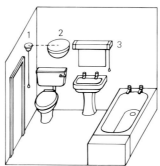

1 Cord-operated light switch **2** Enclosed lampholder **3** Mirror light with built-in isolated shaver socket **4** Cord-operated, wall-mounted heater **5** Cord-operated, shower heater switch **6** Shower unit connected to separate fuse **7** Heated towel rail wired to fused connection unit outside bathroom

VENTILATION

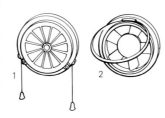

1 Window ventilator **2** Window ventilator and fan

2 *In this elegant white bathroom each element has been carefully chosen to stand out against the plainest of backgrounds. The basin is a beautiful pedestal; there is lovely old free-standing furniture and two decorative figures stand between the sophisticated brass and glass lights. An old-fashioned, solid, curvy radiator fits into the room perfectly. It also offers plenty of warmth.*

3 *One advantage of leaving the pipes on show in a bathroom is that hot pipes can assist with heating the room. To look attractive, they must be part of the decorative scheme. Otherwise it appears that the pipes are merely badly installed. In this bathroom they are made part of the scheme because of the free-standing traditional claw-footed bath and the old-style basin hung on the wall with its pipes on view. This basin is not only highly attractive to look at, but also practical to use because its built-in back and winged sides prevent water splashing. Hot pipes do not provide sufficient heat for the whole room and are supplemented here by a low-level modern radiator which tucks in neatly below the window.*

INDEX

Page numbers in *italic* refer to
illustrations and captions

ACKNOWLEDGEMENTS

The publisher thanks the following photographers and organizations for their kind permission to reproduce the photographs and artwork in this book:

Abitare (Gabriele Basilico) **24** *1*; Behr Furniture **23** *3*; Vivian Boje **31** *3*; Camera Press **18** *2*, **19** *6*, **20-1**, **23** *2*, **24** *2*, **32** *1*, **36** *1*, **44** *1*, **46** *2*, **48** *3*, **50** *1*, **51** *3* and *4*, **52** *1*, *2* and *3*, **53** *5* and *8*, **60** *1*, **61** *6*, **64** *1* and *3*, **69** *4*, **70-1**, **72** *1*, **75** *4* and *6*; courtesy Conran's U.S.A. **6** *1*, **30** *1*; Gilles de Chabaneix **8** *1*, **63** *5*, **67** *6*; Council of British Sanitaryware Manufacturers (Allia, Armitage Shanks, Ideal-Standard, Johnson Brothers, Shires Bathrooms and Twyfords Bathrooms) **58-9** (plans); Dorma **9** *6*, **22-3** *1*; Dux Interiors Ltd **8** *2*; D.D. Flicker Ltd **14-15** *1*; Gautier **46** *3*; Good Housekeeping (Jan Baldwin) **28** *2*, **34-5** (David Brittain) **67** *3* and *5*, **69** *3* (David Montgomery) **16** *2* (Malcolm Robertson) **24-5** *3*; Susan Griggs Agency/Michael Boys **18** *1*, **61** *4*; Kari Haavisto **15** *3*; Habitat **6** *2*, **9** *4* and *5*, **16-17** *3*, **28** *1*, **39** *2*, **46** *1*, **53** *6*, **66** *1* and *2*; Robert Harding/Brock **73** *2*; C.P. Hart & Sons Ltd **64** *2*; Hilary's Quilts **1**; Maison Française (Jaques Primois) **37** *2* (Monsieur Gervais) **62** *1*; La Maison de Marie Claire (Nicolas/Pelle) **4-5** (Eriaud/A.M. Comte) **12-13**, **42-3** (Korniluff/Billaud) **19** *4* (Nicolas/N Vallery-Radot) **19** *5* (Godeaut/Belmont) **26-7**, **68** *1*, **77** *2* (Hussenot/Charras) **39** *3*, **73** *5* (Pons/Puech) **47** *4* (Eriaud/Postic) **48-9**, **51** *2* (Dirand) **54-5** (Kukhan/Hirshnani) **56** *1*, **57** *2* (Rozès/C Hirsch-Marie) **63** *3*, **67** *4* (Bouchet/S. Hourdin) **77** *3*; Bent Rej **7** *3*, **8** *3*, **15** *2*, **33** *3*, **39** *4*, **48** *1* and *2*; Terry Sims **45** *4*; Handpainted bedrooms by Smallbone **31** *2*; John Vaughan **38** *1*; Deidi von Schaewen **63** *4*; Elizabeth Whiting & Associates (Michael Dunne) **16** *1*, **29** *3*, **76** *1* (Home Improvement) **47** *5* (Rodney Hyett) **74** *1* and *3* (Neil Lorimer) **75** *5* (Michael Nicholson) **60** *3* (Spike Powell) **61** *5*, **65** *4* (Tim Street-Porter) **63** *2* (Jerry Tubby) **53** *7*, **73** *4*, **74** *2* (Andrea von Einsiedel) **60** *2*; Shona Wood (designer Chris Hall) **68** *2*.

The following photographs were taken especially for Conran Octopus:
Bill Batten (designer Hilary Green) **40** *1*; David Brittain (Ken Lumsdale, furniture Mothercare UK Limited) **45** *2* and *3*; Simon Brown **41** *3*, **52** *4* (architect Richard Gooden) **41** *2* (architect Ian Hutchinson) **73** *3*; Ken Kirkwood (designer George Powers) **18** *3* (architect Roger Mears) **33** *2*.

Source material for the following illustrations was supplied by Homebase:
25, **31**, **45**, **49**, **56-7**, **61**, **63**, **65**, **69**, **72-3**.

●●●●